Kevin Love

by **Marty Gitlin**

Consultant: Jon Krawczynski
AP Basketball Writer

BEARPORT
PUBLISHING

New York, New York

Credits

Cover and Title Page, © Mark Duncan/AP Images, Marcio Jose Sanchez/AP Images, and Casey Rodgers/AP Images for Time Warner Cable; 4, © Mark J. Terrill/AP Images; 5, © Jon SooHoo/UPI/Newscom; 6, © Kevin Reece/Icon Sportswire; 7, © Steve Boyle/Corbis; 8, © Ric Tapia/Icon Sportswire; 9, © Sporting News/ZUMA Press/Icon Sportswire; 10, © Lucas Jackson/Reuters/Newscom; 11, © Allen Fredrickson/Icon Sportswire; 12, © Jim Mone/AP Images; 13, © Friso Gentsch/dpa/picture-alliance/Newscom; 14, © Photo Image/Shutterstock; 15, © David Sherman/NBAE via Getty Images; 16, © Darrell Walker/Icon SMI/Newscom; 17, © Paul Spinelli/AP Images; 18, © Mark Sauer/Mesabi Daily News/AP Images; 19, © David Sherman/NBAE via Getty Images; 20, © Ezra Acayan/Sipa USA/Newscom; 21, © David Richard/USA Today Sports/Newscom; 22, © Staff/MCT/Newscom.

Publisher: Kenn Goin
Senior Editor: Joyce Tavolacci
Creative Director: Spencer Brinker
Photo Researcher: Chrös McDougall

Library of Congress Cataloging-in-Publication Data

Gitlin, Marty.
  Kevin Love / by Marty Gitlin.
    p. cm. (Basketball heroes making a difference)
  Includes bibliographical references and index.
  ISBN 978-1-62724-548-7 (library binding) — ISBN 1-62724-548-0 (library binding)
  1. Love, Kevin, 1988—Juvenile literature. 2. Basketball players—United States—Biography—Juvenile literature. I. Title.
  GV884.L65G57 2015
  796.323092—dc23
  [B]
                              2014034564

For more information, write to Bearport Publishing Company, Inc., 45 West 21st Street, Suite 3B, New York, New York 10010. Printed in the United States of America.

10 9 8 7 6 5 4 3 2 1

Contents

The Big Shot 4

Growing Up with Hoops 6

College Star 8

Timberwolves Time 10

Becoming a Superstar 12

Kevin's Coat Drive 14

Joining a Big Battle 16

Taking the Plunge 18

New Team, New Town 20

The Kevin File 22

Glossary 23

Bibliography 24

Read More 24

Learn More Online 24

Index 24

The Big Shot

It was January 20, 2012, and the Minnesota Timberwolves and LA Clippers were tied 98–98. Timberwolves **power forward** Kevin Love heard the fans cheering for their home team, the Clippers. "Defense! Defense! Defense!" the fans yelled. Time was running out, and Minnesota had the ball. Kevin knew that he needed to score.

With one second remaining, Kevin received a pass. He quickly shot a **three-pointer** just before the buzzer sounded. *Swish!* The basket gave the Timberwolves a 101–98 win! This was not the first time Kevin had led his team to victory.

Kevin celebrates his game-winning shot against the Clippers.

Kevin leaps high into the air to make the three-point shot against the Clippers.

Kevin makes a lot of three-pointers despite being a power forward. Most power forwards stay closer to the basket.

Growing Up with Hoops

Thanks to his family, Kevin started playing hoops at an early age. Kevin Wesley Love was born on September 7, 1988, in Santa Monica, California. A year later, his family moved to Lake Oswego, Oregon. Kevin's dad, Stan Love, had played in the **NBA** and helped Kevin learn all about basketball. "He taught me basically everything I know," Kevin said.

Kevin spent hours practicing shooting, passing, and **rebounding** skills. Those fundamentals helped him become a strong player later on. During high school, he led his team to the state championship game three years in a row. In his junior year, Kevin helped his team win the Oregon state title!

Wes Unseld (#41) played with Stan Love in the NBA. Growing up, Kevin learned how to get rebounds by watching videos of Unseld.

Kevin averaged 26.8 points and 14.5 rebounds per game during his four years at Lake Oswego High School in Oregon.

As a high school senior, six-foot-ten-inch- (2.1 m) tall Kevin was named the 2007 Gatorade High School National Player of the Year.

College Star

After Kevin finished high school, colleges from across the country offered him basketball **scholarships**. Fans at the nearby University of Oregon hoped Kevin would play there, just like his dad had done. They were disappointed, however, when Kevin decided to play for the University of California, Los Angeles (UCLA) Bruins instead. Kevin said UCLA just felt like the best fit.

In college, Kevin no longer towered over the other players. Yet he was able to make baskets from any position on the court. Plus, his quickness helped him grab rebounds over taller players. In fact, no Bruins player had more rebounds than Kevin. So it's no wonder that Kevin led his new team to the **Final Four** when he was just a freshman.

Kevin averaged 17.5 points and 10.6 rebounds per game as a freshman at UCLA.

As a freshman, Kevin earned the Pacific-12 Conference Men's Basketball Player of the Year award.

Even though Kevin (right) scored 12 points and had 9 rebounds, UCLA lost to the University of Memphis in the 2008 Final Four.

Timberwolves Time

In just one year, Kevin had proven that he was one of the best players in college basketball. At that point, he decided he was ready to test his skills against the world's best and entered the NBA **draft** in 2008. Draft night had its twists and turns, however. Kevin was selected fifth overall by the Memphis Grizzlies. Then, in a sudden shake-up, the Minnesota Timberwolves traded for him.

Soon after Kevin joined the Timberwolves, he showed his team what a great player he was. Kevin was not as tall as other NBA power forwards. Yet he made up for that with his strength and attitude. When a shot banged off the basket, he charged at the ball to get the rebound. On **offense**, Kevin became a threat with his accurate shooting and pinpoint passing.

Kevin was a member of the Grizzlies for about five hours before being traded.

One of Kevin's nicknames is K-Love.

Kevin led all **rookies** in **double-doubles** in the 2008–2009 season.

Becoming a Superstar

Kevin showed a lot of promise in his first and second years in the NBA. In his third year, his confidence as a player grew, and he became a star. While shooting more three-pointers than ever, Kevin averaged 20.2 points per game in the 2010–2011 season. Plus, no NBA player averaged more than his 15.2 rebounds per game. It was no surprise that he made his first **All-Star Game** that year.

The next summer, Kevin was a key player for Team USA, helping the squad win an Olympic gold medal in basketball. For three more seasons, he continued to be one of the Timberwolves' best players. Kevin's ability to shoot, rebound, and pass made him a standout on the court.

Kevin's 31 points and 31 rebounds helped the Timberwolves beat the New York Knicks 112–103 in a 2010 game.

In 2010, Kevin became the first player in 28 years to record at least 30 points and 30 rebounds in the same game.

Kevin dunks during the 2012 Olympic gold-medal game.

Kevin's Coat Drive

In addition to being a great ball player, Kevin is a caring member of the community. When he moved to Minneapolis to play for the Timberwolves, he was struck by how cold the winters there are. He also quickly learned that freezing winter temperatures can be dangerous for people without warm clothes.

So during his rookie year, Kevin joined forces with the Salvation Army to collect warm coats. Kevin personally helped deliver the coats to people around the city. Each year, Kevin's coat drive became more and more successful. In 2008, the drive collected around 400 coats. In 2013, that number jumped to more than 4,500 coats!

The average temperature in January in Minneapolis is only 16°F (-9°C).

Kevin was very impressed by how many Timberwolves fans **donated** winter coats to the drive. So starting in 2012, he thanked them by giving away free tickets to a basketball game.

Kevin delivers coats to the Salvation Army in 2012.

Joining a Big Battle

As Kevin grew more popular as a player, he wanted to become even more active in the community. So in October 2012, he decided to find new ways to reach out and help others. He called his efforts "Spread Love."

The first act of Spread Love was to raise awareness of breast cancer and the fight against it. Kevin felt strongly about this cause after a friend learned she had the disease. He decided to take action by donating 25 cents every time someone expressed support for the cause on **social media**. Over about two months, the change added up to $43,000. Kevin then donated the money to Bright Pink, a Chicago organization that helps breast cancer survivors.

Approximately 40,000 women die each year from breast cancer in the United States. Awareness of the disease is symbolized by a pink ribbon.

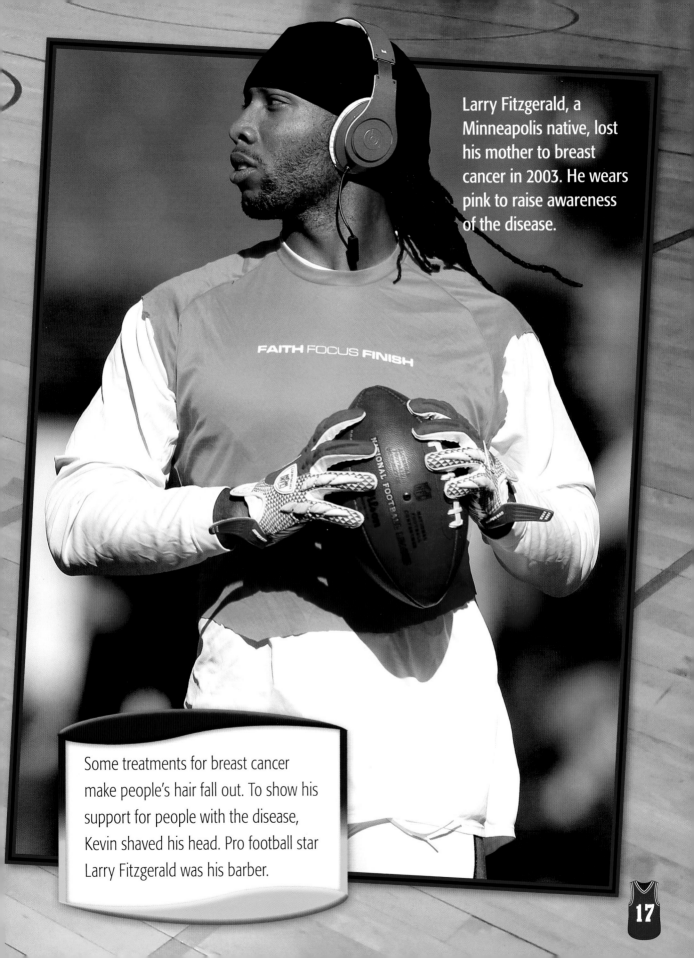

Larry Fitzgerald, a Minneapolis native, lost his mother to breast cancer in 2003. He wears pink to raise awareness of the disease.

FAITH FOCUS FINISH

Some treatments for breast cancer make people's hair fall out. To show his support for people with the disease, Kevin shaved his head. Pro football star Larry Fitzgerald was his barber.

Taking the Plunge

While playing for Minnesota, Kevin also developed a passion for supporting kids who love sports. That's how he found himself on the shores of a nearly frozen lake on March 9, 2013.

That day, along with more than 670 other people, Kevin jumped into the freezing water as part of the state's yearly Polar Bear Plunge. The event raises awareness and money for **Special Olympics** Minnesota. This organization offers kids and adults with intellectual disabilities opportunities to play and compete in sports. Kevin knew that more people would attend the Polar Bear Plunge if an NBA star was there. He was right. The cold-water plunge raised more than $100,000.

An athlete showing off a Special Olympics medal earned in Minnesota

Kevin (center) jumps into Riley Lake for the Polar Bear Plunge. Timberwolves mascot Crunch (left) joined him.

Kevin also helps raise money for St. Jude Children's Research Hospital. The Tennessee hospital and research center provides free medical care for very sick children.

New Team, New Town

Today, Kevin continues to play his hardest and has a fierce desire to win on the court. However, after six seasons with the Timberwolves, he decided he wanted a fresh start with another team. In the summer of 2014, Kevin was traded to the Cleveland Cavaliers. On the team, he would join forces with LeBron James, another superstar NBA player. "More than anything, I'm just excited to start my time in Cleveland, get to work with my new teammates, and start with this new family here," Kevin told reporters after the trade was announced.

People in Cleveland were excited to have Kevin play there, too. They knew their team was getting a player who not only gives his all on the court but also makes an all-out effort in the community.

Kevin helps a young fan spin a basketball.

When Kevin joined the Cavaliers, he decided to switch from number 42 to number 0. "I thought this was a chance to start fresh," he said.

Kevin shows off his new Cleveland Cavaliers jersey before the 2014–2015 season.

The Kevin File

Kevin is a basketball hero on and off the court. Here are some highlights.

During the 2010–2011 season, the NBA gave Kevin its Most Improved Player award, and he received a free car. Kevin decided to donate the car to the Dylan Witschen Foundation, which raises money for organizations that look for a cure for cancer.

Kevin comes from a famous family. His uncle, Mike Love, is an original member of The Beach Boys.

University of Oregon fans booed Kevin when he returned to his home state as a member of the UCLA basketball team. They were angry that he had left Oregon to play for the Bruins. Kevin responded with 26 points and 18 rebounds to lead his team to a victory over Oregon's team, the Ducks.

Glossary

All-Star Game (AWL-STAR GAYM) a yearly game between the best players in the NBA's Eastern Conference and Western Conference

donated (DOH-nayt-id) gave something to a cause

double-doubles (DUHB-uhl-DUHB-uhlz) having a double-digit statistic in two categories, such as points and rebounds, during one game

draft (DRAFT) an event in which professional teams take turns choosing college athletes to play for them

Final Four (FYE-nuhl FOR) the semifinals of the National Collegiate Athletic Association (NCAA) college basketball championships; the stage of the basketball tournament where only four teams remain in competition

NBA (EN BEE AY) letters standing for the *National Basketball Association*, the professional men's basketball league in North America

offense (AW-fenss) the team that has possession of the ball and is trying to score

power forward (POU-ur FOR-wurd) a position on a basketball team that often plays close to the hoop and requires strong defense and rebounding

rebounding (REE-bound-ing) catching balls after a missed shot

rookies (RUK-ees) first-year players

scholarships (SKOL-ur-ships) money given to people for education

social media (SOH-shuhl MEE-dee-uh) Web sites in which people interact with other people or organizations

Special Olympics (SPESH-uhl oh-LIM-piks) a group that organizes athletic events for children and adults who have intellectual disabilities

three-pointer (three-POINT-ur) a long-distance shot that is worth three points

Bibliography

Branch, John. "Having Fun, Fun, Fun as a Freshman at U.C.L.A." *New York Times* (March 18, 2008).

Clemmons, Anna Katherine. "Kevin Love's Coat Drive Warms Twin Cities." ESPN.com (December 14, 2012).

Jenkins, Lee. "Love Is In the Air." *Sports Illustrated* (December 20, 2010).

www.NBA.com

Read More

Fishman, Jon M. *Kevin Love (Amazing Athletes).* Minneapolis, MN: Lerner (2014).

Gitlin, Marty. *Cleveland Cavaliers (Inside the NBA).* Edina, MN: ABDO (2012).

Goessling, Ben. *Minnesota Timberwolves (Inside the NBA).* Edina, MN: ABDO (2012).

Learn More Online

To learn more about Kevin Love and the Cleveland Cavaliers, visit
www.bearportpublishing.com/BasketballHeroes

Index

Bright Pink 16

Cleveland Cavaliers 20–21

coat drive 14–15

family 6, 8, 22

Fitzgerald, Larry 17

James, LeBron 20

Love, Stan 6, 8

Memphis Grizzlies 10

Minneapolis, Minnesota 14, 17

Minnesota Timberwolves 4, 10, 12, 14–15, 19, 20

Olympics 12–13

Polar Bear Plunge 18–19

Salvation Army 14–15

Special Olympics Minnesota 18

St. Jude Children's Research Hospital 19

University of California, Los Angeles (UCLA) 8–9, 22

Unseld, Wes 6